The Story of Macbeth

Shakespeare's play retold

by Philip Hewitt

Ernst Klett Verlag
Stuttgart Düsseldorf Leipzig

Picture credits
Corbis, Düsseldorf: p. 3 (Hellier), p. 6 (Gillian Darley)
defd, Hamburg: cover
Matthias Stark, Fernwald-Annerod: map p. 14

1. Auflage 1 5 4 3 2 1 | 2007 06 05 04 03

Alle Drucke dieser Auflage können im Unterricht nebeneinander benutzt werden. Die letzte Zahl bezeichnet das Jahr dieses Druckes.

Internetadresse: http://www.klett-verlag.de

Druck: Medien Druck, Unterland
Printed in Germany.
ISBN 3-12-530510-1

LIST OF CHARACTERS

The Royal House of Scotland

DUNCAN	King of Scotland
MALCOLM	his elder son
DONALBAIN	his younger son

Thanes (noblemen of Scotland) their households and supporters

MACBETH Thane of Glamis later Thane of Cawdor later King of Scotland	BANQUO
LADY MACBETH	FLEANCE Banquo's son
LADY-IN-WAITING her attendant	MACDUFF Thane of Fife
SEYTON Macbeth's armour bearer	LADY MACDUFF
PORTER at Macbeth's castle	
AN OLD MAN	ROSS, LENNOX, MENTEITH, ANGUS, CAITHNESS — other thanes
DOCTOR	
MURDERERS	

The supernatural world

THREE WITCHES the weird sisters	HECATE Queen of Witchcraft
THREE APPARITIONS	

The English

SIWARD Earl of Northumberland
YOUNG SIWARD his son

Lords, Ladies, Servants, Messenger, Soldiers

The play is set in Scotland and England.

The Story of Macbeth

The New Globe was reconstructed near the original site of Shakespeare's Globe. The faithful reconstruction took years to complete, most of the money coming from donations. The Globe was opened by Queen Elizabeth II in 1997.

Act One

An open place

It was a stormy night in a wild and lonely part of Scotland. Lightning was flashing and thunder was crashing. Heavy rain was falling. It was not a night to be outside, and most people were indoors, sitting close to their fires.

Nobody saw the three old women talking together on the open heath, nobody heard that they were planning to meet again soon. This was just as well, for the three women were witches, as wild as the stormy night. Witches? Well, a thousand years ago, when this story took place, there were still monsters and witches in that part of the world.

These were stormy times. Scotland was at war. The witches knew that there would be a battle the following day. The Scottish king's army led by Macbeth, Thane of Glamis, and his friend Banquo would be fighting an army of Scottish rebels led by the Thane of Cawdor and helped by the King of Norway and his troops.

"When shall we three meet again?" asked the first witch.

"When the battle's lost and won," said the second.

"Where?" asked the first witch.

"Upon the heath," replied the second.

"There to meet with Macbeth," said the third witch. Because they had news for Macbeth. Good news and bad news. A strange mixture of both.

First Witch:	When shall we three meet again? In thunder, lightning or in rain?
Second Witch:	When the hurly-burly's done, When the battle's lost and won.

---

6 **heath** [hi:θ] area of flat, unused land, often covered by heather ['heθə] *(= Heidekraut)* – 7 **witch** woman who can work magic *(Hexe)* – 13 **Thane** [θeɪn] aristocratic title (originally a man who performed military service for his king in return for land) – 14 **rebel** ['rebəl]

Third Witch:	That will be ere the set of sun.
First Witch:	Where the place?
Second Witch:	Upon the heath.
Third Witch:	There to meet with Macbeth.

King Duncan's camp near Forres

It had been a hard battle. Sometimes it had seemed that the Scottish king's enemies would win, but after much heavy fighting, "Brave Macbeth", as people called him, had managed to kill the rebel Macdonwald and defeat his army. The Norwegians attacked again, but Macbeth and Banquo had led King Duncan's army to victory.

The king was so happy to hear that the rebellious Thane of Cawdor had been taken prisoner that he decided to give Macbeth, who was his cousin, Cawdor's title and lands.

"Execute the traitor Cawdor," said the king. "What he has lost, noble Macbeth has won."

A heath

As they had promised the night before, the three witches were waiting for Macbeth on the heath near the battlefield. While they waited, they talked and laughed about the nasty things they had done in the last few days.

It was Banquo who saw the three old women first, and he was so shocked by their looks that he could hardly believe that they were human.

"Speak if you can," said Macbeth. "What are you?"

---

ere ['ɪə] before – 10 **to execute** ['eksəkju:t] to kill a person as a punishment – **traitor** ['treɪtə] person who commits a crime against the state *(Verräter)* – 11 **noble** showing high character; of high birth

But instead of answering his question, they greeted him with their news.

"All hail Macbeth! Hail, Thane of Glamis!" said the first witch.

"All hail Macbeth! Hail, Thane of Cawdor!" said the second, greeting him with his new title. But it was the third witch who had the most surprising news:

"All hail Macbeth! You shall be king one day!"

Macbeth was shocked by this prophecy. After all, he had just defeated one rebel as one of the king's faithful generals and must have known that the only way he could become King of Scotland quickly would be to become a rebel himself: he would first have to kill his cousin Duncan and possibly also Malcolm and Donalbain, Duncan's two sons.

But although these thoughts shocked him, as they would have shocked any noble and faithful person, he was not only a brave soldier but also an ambitious man. He knew that his wife was even more ambitious. King of Scotland? With her as queen? Why not?

But the three witches also had news for Banquo. They said that although he himself would never become king, his children would.

"Lesser than Macbeth, and greater," said the first witch, with a smile.

"Not so happy, yet much happier," said the second. And before the astonished men could ask where they got their information from, the three witches disappeared, leaving Macbeth and Banquo to think about their prophecies.

The first prophecy was fulfilled almost immediately. Out of the darkness walked the Thanes of Ross and Angus with the news that the king had made Macbeth Thane of Cawdor.

Even if Macbeth had never thought that he might become king before his meeting with the three witches, the fulfilment of their first prophecy made him believe that it was his destiny, his fate to become king.

---

1 **to greet sb** to say hello and to welcome – 3 **all hail** [heɪl] form of greeting or welcome to an important person – **Glamis** [glɑ:mz] famous castle in eastern Scotland, birthplace of the late Queen Mother – 8 **prophecy** ['prɒfəsɪ] – 9 **faithful** loyal and true – 16 **ambitious** [æm'bɪʃəs] full of a strong wish to do well *(ehrgeizig)* – 20 **lesser** (of two people) not so great as the other person – 23 **astonished** [ə'stɒnɪʃt] surprised – 31 **destiny** power believed to control events or a person's future and which cannot be resisted *(Schicksal)* **fate** destiny

'If chance will have me king, why, chance will crown me,' he thought, as he followed the others to find the king. The only thing that worried him was what the witches had said about Banquo's future. If he, Macbeth, was to become king then surely his own sons should be kings after him! Turning to Banquo, he said they must talk about what had happened at a more suitable time. Neither of them knew that events would soon move so quickly that they would never find time for their little chat.

King Duncan's palace at Forres

There was good reason for celebration at the royal palace at Forres that night. King Duncan, his sons Malcolm and Donalbain and other courtiers discussed the situation, particularly the execution of the traitor Cawdor.

"He died like a gentleman," said Malcolm.

"He was a gentleman whom I trusted absolutely," his father replied.

Just as he was saying this, Macbeth and Banquo arrived. Duncan was very glad to see his cousin Macbeth, who spoke modestly about his part in the victory. He was, after all, only doing his duty, as a loyal and faithful servant of the king.

Duncan had already richly rewarded Macbeth with the title and lands of the unhappy Cawdor. There were no generous rewards for the faithful Banquo. Turning to his eldest son Malcolm, Duncan made a spontaneous decision that would have serious consequences: "You will be the next King of Scotland, Malcolm. From now on you will have the title Prince of Cumberland."

In those days it was not always the eldest son who became king

---

9 **celebration** party given to show that something good has happened – 11 **courtier** ['kɔ:tɪə] person who spends much of his or her time at court with the king or queen *(Höfling)* – 14 **to trust** to believe in the honesty or reliability of sb or s.th. – 18 **modest** not showing too high an opinion of oneself or one's abilities *(bescheiden)* – 19 **servant** person who works in the house of a richer person – 21 **generous** ['dʒenərəs] ready to give freely; *here:* large *(großzügig)* – 22 **eldest** oldest (child, brother, sister)

on his father's death. Macbeth's claim to the throne, as Duncan's cousin, was greatly weakened by this new development.

As Duncan had decided to travel on to Macbeth's castle at Inverness, Macbeth hurried off ahead of the royal party to tell his wife about the king's visit. He had already written her a letter telling her what had happened – including the witches' prophecies – and had sent a messenger off with it, ordering him to ride as fast as he could, for this was important news indeed.

Macbeth's castle at Inverness

They say that behind every great man there is an even greater woman. Lady Macbeth could certainly have been described as ambitious, ruthless, unscrupulous and tough.

In his letter, Macbeth had already told his wife how the first of the witches' prophecies had already been fulfilled. She was excited about the idea that her husband might become King – and she Queen – of Scotland, but was worried that Macbeth might be to weak or kind-hearted to do what would be necessary.

She still had her husband's letter in her hand when another messenger came in with the news: "The King comes here tonight. And your noble husband will be here shortly."

Here, indeed was a golden opportunity to achieve her ambitions for her husband and, of course, for herself. By spending the night at their castle, Duncan would be in their power. If only she were a man! Lady Macbeth was still deep in thought when Macbeth arrived at the castle.

"My dearest love. As the messenger told you, Duncan comes here tonight," he said as he entered the room.

"When does he intend to leave?"

"Tomorrow."

---

1 **claim** statement of a right to something *(Anspruch)* – 7 **messenger** ['mesəndʒə] person who carries a message – 11 **ruthless** ['ru:θləs] cruel; not caring about other people's feelings – **unscrupulous** [ʌn'skru:pjʊləs] not held back by one's conscience from doing wrong *(skrupellos)* 20 **ambition** [æm'bɪʃn] a strong wish to be successful, to reach a certain aim 27 **to intend to do s.th.** to have the wish to do s.th.

But Lady Macbeth had already decided that the king would never leave Inverness Castle alive!

"You must play the part of the perfect host," she said. "Hide your feelings, try not to lose the king's favour by any suspicious behaviour. Leave all the rest to me."

In front of Macbeth's castle in Inverness

When the king, his two sons, Banquo and other noblemen arrived at Macbeth's castle in Inverness, near the sea, the air was sweet and fresh, birds were busy at their nests. There was no hint of the coming tragedy.

Lady Macbeth greeted her guest, showing none of her true thoughts.

"Fair and noble hostess," said Duncan. "I am your guest tonight. Give me your hand. Lead me to my host. We love him highly."

Near the great hall in Macbeth's castle

That evening, Macbeth gave a banquet in honour of his noble guest. Already he was beginning to have second thoughts about the planned assassination. He walked out of the castle hall, where the king was still dining, in order to be alone with his thoughts.

'If only it could be done quickly,' he thought. 'If only murdering the king could be the beginning and the end of the whole matter… Duncan is a relative of mine. He is my king and I am his man. He

---

3 **host, hostess** [həʊstəs] man, woman who entertains guests – 4 **suspicious** acting in a way that makes people feel that you cannot be trusted *(verdächtig)* – 12 **fair** *here:* lovely; attractive – 15 **banquet** ['bæŋkwɪt] big meal for a large number of people, often held as part of a celebration – 16 **second thoughts** doubts *(Zweifel)* – 17 **assassination** [əˌsæsɪ'neɪʃn] killing a person for political reasons

is also my guest. He is not even a bad ruler – no one will thank me for killing him. My only motivation is my ambition.'

When Lady Macbeth came out to see where her husband had gone, she was shocked to see how close he was to changing his mind.

"I can't go on with it," he said. "Duncan has honoured me so much and everyone has a good opinion of me. How can I possibly become a traitor, like Cawdor, the man I've only just beaten in battle?"

"You call yourself a man?" was her angry reply. "Why did you tell me about the witches' second prophecy if you had no intention of making it come true? This is our big chance. Listen to my plan: there will only be two men guarding Duncan's bedroom. I will give them enough wine to make them drunk. Then we will use their own daggers to kill the king, wipe Duncan's blood on the drunken guards' clothes so that everyone thinks that Duncan's own servants have killed him. Who would dare to suspect anyone else? And anyway, we'll show our grief and anger at his death. What do you think?"

"All right," agreed Macbeth. "I'll do it."

---

13 **to guard** to look after; to keep safe – 14 **drunk** having drunk so much alcohol that one cannot think or act normally – 15 **dagger** short sword or long knife, used as a weapon – **to wipe** to remove liquid, dust etc. from something with a cloth – 17 **to suspect sb** [sə'spekt] to think that sb has done s.th. – 18 **grief** strong feeling of sadness or unhappiness – **anger** ['æŋgə] strong feeling that makes people want to fight *(Zorn)*

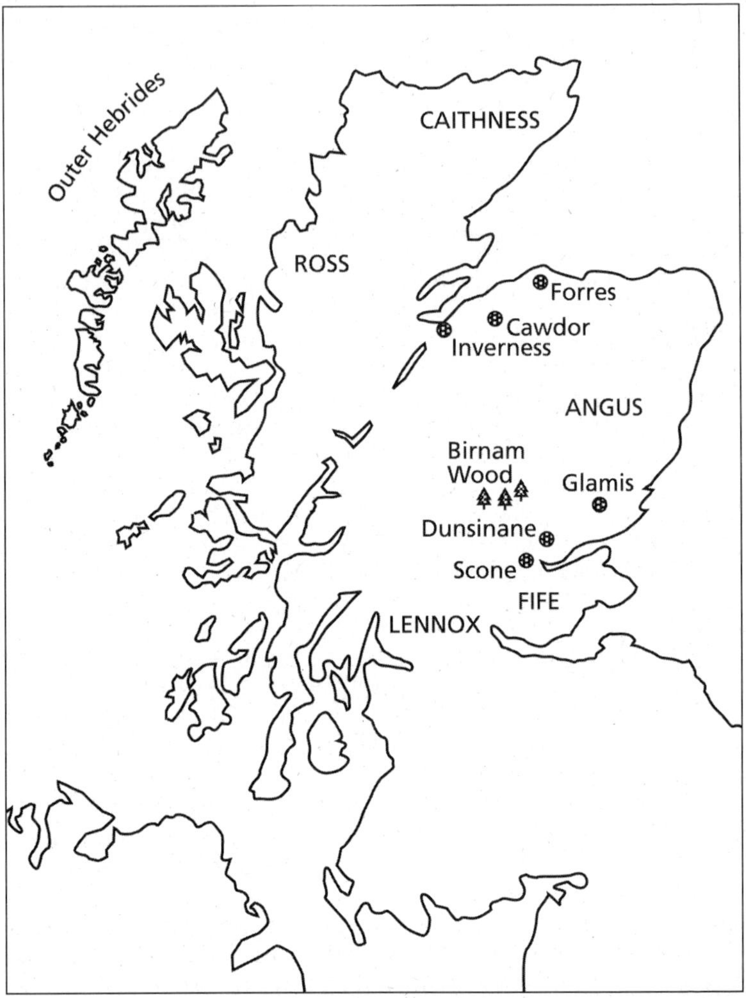

A map of Macbeth's Scotland. It also shows (in capitals) the territory of the thanes.

Court of Macbeth's castle

After their meeting with the witches, Banquo had been finding it hard to sleep. The previous night he had dreamt about their prophecies. So before going to bed tonight, he decided to go outside into the castle courtyard with his son Fleance for some fresh air. He was surprised to see Macbeth still awake long after midnight.

"The king's in bed. He had a wonderful evening and is full of praise for your wife. What a fine hostess she is!" said Banquo, not realizing that Lady Macbeth had just persuaded her husband to go ahead with the terrible murder they had planned. "I dreamt last night of the three witches."

"I never think about them," lied Macbeth. "But we must talk about what they told us whenever you can find the time."

"Whenever you like," Banquo replied.

"Sleep well," said Macbeth, hoping that Banquo and his son Fleance would be in bed before the time came to put Lady Macbeth's plan into action.

Turning to his servant, he told him to go to bed, too. "But tell your mistress to ring the bell when my drink is ready."

Alone in the dark courtyard, Macbeth was still worrying about the planned murder when he suddenly had a vision of a dagger, hanging in the air in front of him:

"Is this a dagger which I see before me, the handle towards my hand?" he whispered to himself, unable to believe what he saw. He put out his hand to get hold of the dagger, but it moved away from him. Was he going crazy? Or was this another sign from the witches that his decision to murder Duncan was the right one?

But there was no time for further thought. A bell rang. This was the signal that his wife had finished preparing for the murder. It reminded Macbeth of the bell which, in those days, was sounded

---

4 **courtyard** piece of open ground (often in a castle) surrounded by buildings – 19 **mistress** female head of the household – 21 **vision** ['vɪʒn] *here:* s.th. seen in the mind's eye

when a body was taken from the church to the churchyard to be buried: the so-called death-knell. This was Duncan's death-knell:

"I go, and it is done. The bell invites me.
Hear it not, Duncan, for it is a knell
That summons thee to heaven, or to hell."

Macbeth's castle – near Duncan's room

Lady Macbeth waited outside in the darkness of the castle courtyard while her husband was inside doing the terrible deed. The two guards were drunk, and she had drunk something, too, to give her the courage she needed to play her part in the murder.

In the silence an owl suddenly cried out, and at first she mistook it for the cry of the murdered king. Then she heard her husband cry out: "Who's there?" and became worried that the assassination plan might have been discovered in spite of all her careful planning. Had she forgotten anything? No. It was a perfect plan.

"I laid their daggers ready," she thought to herself. "He could not miss them." She had gone into the king's bedroom and would have killed Duncan herself if he had not, in sleep, looked so much like her own long-dead father!

At last Macbeth returned, obviously badly shaken but able to greet his wife with the words: "I have done the deed."

Suddenly they heard a cry from inside the castle.

"Who was sleeping in the second room?" asked Macbeth, wondering if someone had raised the alarm already.

"Donalbain."

Looking down at his bloodstained hands, Macbeth told his wife how he had heard the guards talking in their sleep. One laughed,

---

1 **churchyard** ground around a church where the dead are buried – 2 **death-knell** church bell which is rung during a burial service – 5 **to summon** to call (usually officially) – **thee** *(old form)* you – 10 **owl** [aʊl] big bird which flies and hunts its food at night – **to mistake, mistook, mistaken** to make a mistake about the identity of sb or s.th. *(fälschlich halten für)* – 25 **bloodstained** covered in or marked with blood

and the other, strangely enough, cried "Murder!" so that they woke each other.

Lady Macbeth tried to calm him down: "Don't worry about these things or they'll drive you mad." Perhaps she should not have mentioned madness, because the next thing Macbeth told her made it look, indeed, as if he was going mad.

"I thought I heard a voice cry 'Sleep no more! Macbeth does murder sleep'."

Macbeth would indeed find it difficult to sleep from that day on. With another look at her husband's bloodstained hands, the practical Lady Macbeth realized that her fool of a husband was still holding the murder weapons and had forgotten to wipe blood on the guards' hands and faces!

"Go get some water," she ordered, "and wash the blood off your hands. Why did you bring these daggers from the place? They must lie there: go take them back and wipe the blood on the sleeping guards' clothes!"

But Macbeth refused. He had had enough for one night. "I'll go no more. I am afraid to think what I have done; I dare not look at it again."

So Lady Macbeth went off to finish the job. When she returned, her hands were as red as her husband's and she was unable to resist one last comment:

"My hands are as red as yours now, but I would be ashamed to have a heart so white!"

Suddenly there was a loud knocking at the south gate of the castle.

"We'd better get back to our bedroom quickly and into our nightclothes," said Lady Macbeth. "It will look strange if we are still fully dressed when the murder is discovered. A quick wash and nobody will suspect us." But her husband was already regretting his deed. When there was another loud knock at the gate he said, half to himself: "Wake Duncan with your knocking! I wish you could!"

If his wife heard his words, she said nothing.

---

3 **to calm sb down** [kɑ:m] to make a person less excited – 5 **madness** state of being mad –

The entrance to Macbeth's castle

It was a while before the sleepy, rather drunk porter finally opened the gate to the courtiers Macduff and Lennox, who had come to wake the king early. They were in no hurry so early in the morning, so they joked with the drunken porter for a while, not realizing what a bloody scene was waiting for them in the king's bedroom.

"Is your master awake?" Macduff asked the porter, but before he could reply Macbeth appeared, dressed in his night clothes, to tell them that the king was not awake yet but that he would take them to the king's bedroom so that Macduff could wake his master.

"What a stormy night!" said Lennox while they were waiting for Macduff to wake the king. "The wind blew our chimney pots down, and some people say they heard strange screams of death and other mysterious noises. Owls were hooting all night – a bad sign!"

"It was a rough night," said Macbeth, remembering his own act of violence. But before he could say anything more, Macduff rushed out of the king's bedroom, his eyes wild with horror, hardly able to speak.

"What's the matter?" asked Macbeth and Lennox at the same time.

"The king has been murdered!"

"I can't believe it!" cried Macbeth, although he knew that it was true.

"Go in and see for yourselves."

Macduff refused to return to the bedroom with the others. His job now was to wake everybody in the house and give them the terrible news.

"Awake, awake!" he shouted. "Ring the alarm bell. Murder and treason! Banquo and Donalbain! Malcolm! Awake!"

---

1 **porter** gatekeeper – 5 **bloody** *(literally)* covered in blood; *(figuratively)* terrible; shocking – 6 **master** male head of the household – 12 **chimney pot** round pot on the top of a chimney through which the smoke passes *(Schornsteinkopf)* – 14 **to hoot** to make the sound an owl makes – 30 **treason** ['tri:zn] crime against the state *(Verrat)*

As if woken by the bell, Lady Macbeth came in and asked what had happened. Not wishing to shock the lady, Macduff refused to answer her question at first. But the next person on the scene was Banquo, and Macduff told him the terrible news: "Our royal master has been murdered."

"What, in our house?" asked Lady Macbeth, trying to sound surprised.

Banquo could not believe his ears, but when Macbeth, Lennox and Ross came out of the king's bedroom, even Banquo had to face the truth.

Macbeth was doing his best to be shocked by the king's murder, wishing that he had died rather than Duncan, when the king's two sons came rushing in, horrified to hear of their father's murder.

"Who killed him?"

"His own guards with their own daggers," was Macbeth's angry reply.

"Where are they? Let them speak!"

"They cannot speak. They are dead."

"Dead? But how? Who killed them?"

"I did," was Macbeth's bold reply. The others stared at him, open-mouthed. "I'm sorry, but I just couldn't stop myself. There lay Duncan, dead and covered in blood; there stood the murderers with blood on their clothes and daggers. I was so angry that I didn't know what I was doing. You would have done the same yourselves..."

Malcolm looked at Donalbain, Donalbain at Malcolm. There was something strange about this murder. Their father killed in his cousin's castle. The guards dead. No witnesses... Malcolm knew that people would suspect him first. After all, Duncan had made him Prince of Cumberland only the day before. Suddenly everyone seemed to be looking at him, until Macduff noticed that Lady Macbeth was about to faint.

"Look to the lady!" he cried, and two servants helped her back to her bedroom.

---

13 **horrified** terribly shocked; filled with horror – 20 **bold** showing no fear – 28 **witness** person who sees s.th. happen – 30 **Prince of Cumberland** title of the person who was to be the next king of Scotland – 32 **to faint** to lose one's senses for a short time after a bad shock *(ohnmächtig werden)*

Banquo, too, suspected treason, but by whom?

He looked quickly across at Malcolm and Donalbain, who seemed strangely unmoved by their father's death. Then he looked at Macbeth. He knew about the witches' prophecy – the others did not. He remembered the little talk which Macbeth had suggested, the 'honours' which Macbeth had promised him. Had he actually killed the king himself? Was Macbeth trying to buy his silence?

"Let us meet in the hall," said Macbeth, "and try to find out what's behind this most bloody piece of work." So they all walked off towards the big hall of the castle – all except Donalbain and Malcolm, who, because they knew that they were innocent, were less impressed by Macbeth's and his wife's performance.

"What will you do?" Malcolm asked his brother. "They think one of us did it. Let's not stay here with them. It's easy for bad people to show a sorrow they do not really feel. There will be plenty of time for us to show our true sorrow later. I'll go to England."

Donalbain had also made a quick decision: "I'm off to Ireland. We'll both be safer if we are as far apart as possible. Where we are now, there are daggers in men's smiles! The closer you are to a blood relation, the more likely he is to want your blood!"

"My horse is quickly saddled," said Malcolm. "No need to say goodbye to the others."

If the two brothers had thought about the matter a little more carefully, they would have realized that their sudden departure, without saying goodbye to their host, would make everybody think that one or both of them had murdered their father. But those were wild times. With the king dead and without powerful friends at court, Donalbain, who had been sleeping in the room next to his father's, was quite right to remember the old saying: 'The nearer in blood, the nearer bloody.'

---

11 **innocent** not having committed a crime, not guilty – 25 **departure** [dɪˈpɑːtʃə] act of leaving

Outside Macbeth's castle

The day after Duncan's murder was almost as dark as the stormy night before. It was as if nature itself was shocked by the unnatural deed. While the Thane of Ross was standing in the courtyard waiting to hear the results of the meeting in the hall, he talked to an old man who had seen much in his long life, but never anything like what had happened the previous night or over the past few days, for that matter.

"It's unnatural," was the old man's comment. "Just like the terrible murder of the king."

When Macduff came down into the courtyard, Ross was surprised to see the mixed feelings on his face.

"Malcolm and Donalbain, the king's two sons, are gone. They have fled, which puts suspicion of the deed upon them."

"I can't believe it," said Ross. "It's so unnatural. Now that Malcolm has fled, Macbeth will probably be the new king."

"He is already named," Macduff replied. "And goes to Scone to be crowned ..."

Scone Abbey was the traditional place where the kings of Scotland were crowned. Ross looked carefully at Macduff before asking his cousin an all-important question: "Will you go to Scone?"

"No, cousin, I'm going home to Fife," was the reply.

Ross made a quick decision: "Well, I will go to Scone."

"I hope you see things well done there: goodbye!" said Macduff. Ross watched his cousin leave with a heavy heart. Both of them knew that Macduff would make an enemy of Macbeth if he stayed away from the coronation. But with Duncan's sons safe in England or Ireland, someone had to take the lead in showing that not everyone in Scotland was happy with the choice of Macbeth as the new king.

---

13 **to flee, fled, fled** to run away – **suspicion** [sə'spɪʃn] feeling that sb is probably guilty of a crime *(Verdacht)* – 27 **coronation** [ˌkɒrə'neɪʃn] ceremony at which a person is crowned, i.e. made king or queen

Act Three

The royal palace at Forres

So King Duncan was dead, murdered by Macbeth with the encouragement and help of his wife. Malcolm and Donalbain had fled – the first to England, the second to Ireland – and Macbeth had succeeded in putting suspicion on the king's sons.

The witches' second prophecy had indeed come true. Macbeth was quickly crowned King and his wife Queen of Scotland.

After the coronation, at the royal palace at Forres, Banquo was doing some hard thinking about his own situation while waiting for the king and queen to arrive from Scone. After all, the witches had had good news for him, too. Would his sons become kings of Scotland? How would this be possible unless he became king first? Perhaps, he thought, it would only be possible at the price of his own death.

And why was Macbeth so anxious to have a private talk with him? Perhaps Macbeth would like to 'do a deal', thought Banquo. But he knew that he could never share Macbeth's bloody deed or dark future. He had, after all, always served Duncan faithfully.

Suddenly Banquo heard the sound of trumpets as King Macbeth and his queen entered the room with Lennox, Ross and other lords and ladies.

"I'm giving a dinner here in the palace this evening," Macbeth said to Banquo. "I expect to see you there."

Banquo was not too keen. He had intended to go riding that afternoon. All the same, the king's invitation definitely sounded like an order. 'How he has changed,' thought Banquo bitterly. 'Only a few days ago we were good friends. Now I have to obey his orders!' But he said: "I'll be there, sir."

Banquo was now the man Macbeth feared most of all. Banquo was the only other person who had heard the prophecies of the three witches. The old women had also promised him that his son

---

2 **encouragement** giving a person the courage to do something – 14 **anxious** ['æŋkʃəs] *here:* very keen, eager – 15 **to do a deal** to promise to do sb a favour in return for a favour from him or her – 26 **to obey** to do what you are told

would become king after Macbeth. He remembered how Banquo had criticized the witches for prophesying that he, Macbeth, would become king. Macbeth suddenly had a terrible thought: 'Have I killed the king only to make it more likely that Banquo's son will become king after me?'

The easiest way to solve the problem, of course, would be to kill Banquo and his son Fleance – two more murders would make Macbeth's position safe. Indeed, Macbeth already had a plan. Not long afterwards, a servant came in with news that two men were waiting to see him. Macbeth had already talked to these men about Banquo. About how Banquo had ruined their lives – or so Macbeth said.

"Come in, gentlemen!" said the king. "Sit down. Have you thought about what we discussed last time? You have good reasons for hating Banquo, and so have I. If he died, you would have your revenge and I, who suffer while he is alive, would be in much better health – and better able," he said, looking carefully at the two men, "to remember my true friends."

The two men looked at each other, then at Macbeth and nodded.

"Good. I see we understand each other. Kill him tonight," ordered the king. "And make sure that his son Fleance shares his father's fate."

A room in the royal palace

Lady Macbeth was not happy about the situation either. At last they had what they wanted: she was queen and her husband was king. But they were unable to enjoy their new power. It seemed to her that they had given everything and received nothing in return.

She was worried about her husband, too. He had been sleeping badly, and seemed very depressed. Perhaps he would be in a better mood at the big banquet that evening. 'What's done, is done,' she

---

11 **to ruin** ['ru:ɪn] to spoil – 29 **depressed** feeling unhappy and in low spirits – 30 **mood** state of one's mind (happy, depressed, sad etc.)

thought. It was too late to go back now anyway. The only way open to them was forward, as the new King and Queen of Scotland.

When Macbeth joined his wife in the hall of the palace, he told her that his thoughts – and dreams – had been of his dark deeds.

"Pull yourself together," said his wife, rather sharply. "Be bright and merry among your guests tonight."

"So I shall, my love, and so should you be. Be especially nice to Banquo." Macbeth did not tell his wife that he had already sent two assassins to murder Banquo and his son. Perhaps he did not want to involve her. Perhaps he wanted to prove that he was not the coward she thought he was. He only hinted that, before night fell, another dreadful deed would have been done.

"Don't ask too many questions," he said. "You'll be pleased enough when you find out what I have arranged. It's nearly time for the banquet. We must not be late for our guests – particularly for our special guest, Banquo!"

A lonely place near the palace

Macbeth was taking no chances that evening. He sent one of his own men to the park near the palace where the two assassins were waiting for Banquo and Fleance. Perhaps he was worried that they might make a mess of the job. The other two were not pleased to discover that Macbeth did not seem to trust them, but accepted the third man's story that the king had sent him to help them.

Darkness was falling. Suddenly the three men heard horses approaching and Banquo's voice calling for a light.

"Here they come!" said the second man, pulling out a sharp dagger.

"Wait! Listen!" cried the first murderer suddenly. "The horses are walking off in the opposite direction!"

---

10 **assassin** murderer – 11 **to involve sb** to make a person share an action, often unwillingly – 12 **coward** ['kaʊəd] person who is afraid, who lacks courage – 25 **to approach** to come closer –

"Don't worry," said the third man. "All riders leave their horses here and walk to the palace gates. So much the better! It wouldn't be easy to attack two men on horses."

It was dark by now, but whoever had taken the horses away had given Banquo and Fleance a torch to light their way back to the palace. Even so, they did not see the three assassins until the moment they were attacked.

Banquo fell, shouting a warning to his son as he died. The torch went out and Fleance was able to escape. The king would not be pleased.

The banqueting hall at Forres

The tables in the great hall were laid for the banquet when Macbeth, his wife, Ross, Lennox and other lords and courtiers came in. Normally, the places at which each guest sat would be strictly arranged by protocol. The greatest lords would sit closest to the king and queen. But that night Macbeth decided to move from table to table for a change, to "mingle with society" as he said to his wife.

But he had his own special reason for wanting to move around the hall: nobody would notice if he left the hall to talk to someone who had not been invited to the banquet – one of the assassins, for example. He was anxious for news, hoping for the best. He welcomed his guests and began to move from table to table, chatting. Almost immediately he caught sight of one of the assassins, waiting in the shadows.

Macbeth moved towards him.

"There's blood on your face!" whispered the king.

"It's Banquo's, then."

"Is he dead?"

"My lord, his throat is cut; that I did for him."

---

5 **torch** long stick covered with tar at one end; when the tar is burning, the torch can be used as a light *(Fackel)* – 16 **to mingle** to mix (usually with a crowd of people) – 29 **throat** front part of the neck

"Well done! And Fleance?"

"Most royal sir, Fleance escaped."

This was bad news for Macbeth. Once again he had risked all and got nothing in return. Yet another death on his conscience. Happy, for the moment, that at least Banquo was dead, he sent the assassin away. He would speak to him again the next day.

"My royal lord," said Lady Macbeth, who had been looking for her husband for several minutes. "You are not looking after our guests. Aren't you hungry?"

With the news of Banquo's assassination, Macbeth's appetite had indeed returned, so he began to look round for somewhere to sit, remarking to Lennox that he was sorry that Banquo had not arrived yet. Lennox asked the king to sit down, pointing to an empty chair at his own table.

"There are no empty seats," said the king.

"Here's a place for you, sir," said Lennox in surprise.

"Where?"

"Here, my good lord." Was the king going blind? Couldn't he see the empty place? But suddenly Lennox saw that Macbeth had turned very pale. "What's the matter, your highness?"

Others at the table stopped eating and talking and began looking at the king, who was staring at an empty chair. For it was only Macbeth who could see the bloody figure on the chair, smiling at him and shaking his head – Banquo's ghost!

Ross was the first to sum up the situation.

"Gentlemen, rise; his highness is not well."

But Lady Macbeth was quick to assure them that nothing was wrong. The king, she said, had suffered such attacks since his youth. "Pay no attention to him or you will annoy him," she said. "Just go on with your meal. He will be all right in a minute."

In a quiet voice, she told her husband to pull himself together. "Are you a man?" she hissed.

"Yes," he replied, "and a brave one to dare to look on something that might shock the devil! Can't you see it?"

---

4 **conscience** ['kɒnʃəns] inner voice which tells us what is good or bad *(Gewissen)* – 20 **pale** almost white (of a person's face); very light (of colours) – **your highness** way of addressing a prince or other very important person – 32 **to hiss** to make a sharp noise like an angry cat

"What? It's only an empty chair!"

And sure enough, when he looked again, there was no sign of the ghost!

Macbeth had hardly had a moment of peace since his decision to murder Duncan. Sleepless nights, a guilty conscience, more bloodshed to make his position stronger and to get rid of his enemies – and now visions and ghosts! Was he going mad?

"Go back to your guests," warned his wife. "Or they will think something is really wrong."

He sat down and did his best to eat, drink and make merry, even offering a toast "to our dear friend Banquo, whom we miss."

It was a mistake. Hardly had he spoken the words than Banquo's ghost appeared again. Once more the king's face grew pale with fear. "Go away!" he cried, to the surprise of everyone in the hall, and again it was left to Lady Macbeth to calm the courtiers by telling them that there was nothing wrong with her husband. To most of those present, however, it appeared that there was, indeed, a lot wrong with the king that night.

The mood of the banquet was no longer merry. Although none of the others present had seen the ghost, it was obvious that the king was unwell, and Lady Macbeth finally had to ask everybody to leave.

"He grows worse and worse. Questions annoy him," she explained. "I'm sorry to have to break up the banquet, but I must ask you all to leave at once."

"Good night; we hope that his majesty will soon be in better health," said Lennox, as he and the others left the hall as quickly as they could.

Still shaken by what he had seen, Macbeth turned to his wife and said: "It will have blood: they say blood will have blood. Banquo is dead, but Macduff didn't come to my coronation and he isn't here tonight! I must keep a careful eye on him – on all of them! I have a paid spy in every nobleman's household. If anyone is against me, it won't be long before I find out! And I must visit

---

6 **bloodshed** killing; *literally:* the spilling of blood – 26 **his majesty** the king – 33 **spy** person who finds out secrets about a person or country and then gives (or sells) this information to another person or country *(Spion)*

those three old witches again to discover what more they know about the future."

"What you really need," said his wife, almost tenderly, "is a good night's sleep." And with that she led him from the empty banqueting hall.

A heath

While the king was fighting for sleep or suffering from bad dreams and waking to the horror of what he had done, the three witches met again on the lonely heath. The thunder of a distant storm greeted them, and flashes of distant lightning lit up their ugly, inhuman faces.

But suddenly a witch even more powerful, even more terrible than themselves appeared: Hecate, the Queen of the Witches, well known even to the ancient Greeks.

If the Scottish witches had expected praise from their mistress for what they had done so far, they were very much mistaken.

"How dare you approach Macbeth with your prophecies without asking me?" Hecate screamed. "A poor job you've made of it so far! Why was I never called to play my part? Macbeth will come to you tomorrow to know his destiny. I, the mistress of our art, will be there, too!"

Poor Scotland! Hardly was one civil war over than another was about to begin. Poor Macbeth! Once Hecate herself took a hand, his fate was sealed. Macbeth would soon have to take even more desperate measures to keep his position as king.

---

3 **tenderly** gently; with love – 9 **distant** a long way away – 12 **Hecate** ['hekəti:] the (Greek) goddess of darkness and the underworld – 23 **his fate was sealed** he was damned *(sein Schicksal war besiegelt)* – 24 **desperate** ['desprət] very serious or dangerous – **measure** ['meʒə] *here:* action

The court

Indeed, Lennox and other Scottish lords were drawing their conclusions about what had happened. Rebellion was already in the air at the court at Forres.

"Strange things have happened," said Lennox to another lord, who shared his opinion. "Good King Duncan showed favour to Macbeth: soon afterwards he was dead. And brave Banquo walked too late. And you may, if you like, say that his son Fleance killed him, because Fleance fled – like Malcolm and Donalbain. Men must not walk too late!" There was bitter irony in his voice. How monstrous it was for Malcolm and for Donalbain to kill their good father! Macbeth was so angry that he killed the two guards who had been the slaves of drink and sleep! Wasn't that noble of him? Yes, and wise, too! Thank god Malcolm, Donalbain and Fleance are still outside Macbeth's power, or they would soon find out what it meant to kill a father!

Lennox, who had not been talking to anyone in particular, now turned to the other courtier with an all important question: "I hear Macduff lives in disgrace: sir, can you tell me where he is now?"

"Malcolm went to the English court, and was received by King Edward. Macduff has joined him there. They intend to ask King Edward for help and also to ask for help from Duncan's brother-in-law, Earl Siward of Northumberland. With their help – and with the help of God above, they will make it possible for us to live in peace again, to sleep soundly at night, free from feasts and banquets with bloody knives, to do faithful homage, and to receive honours from a true king!" Looking round to make sure no one else was listening, he went on. "When Macbeth heard that Macduff had gone, he was so angry that he immediately began to prepare for war."

---

1 **to draw a conclusion** to develop a belief or opinion from reliable evidence – 3 **court** group of people (courtiers) who spend much of their time with the monarch at his or her palace – 13 **wise** clever and sensible – 18 **to live in disgrace** [dɪsˈgreɪs] to have lost someone's favour or trust – 22 **earl** [ɜːl] title of a nobleman *(Graf)* – 24 **to sleep soundly** to have a healthy, undisturbed sleep – 25 **homage** [ˈhɒmɪdʒ] act of recognizing the monarch as one's master

Things were indeed going from bad to worse for Scotland and Macbeth. Lennox nodded wisely. For him, help from England could not come too soon. "I hope that some angel will fly to the court of England and bring Macduff's message even before the man himself arrives. Macbeth is a curse on our country!"

"I'll send my prayers with your angel!" said the other with deeper feeling than he would have dared to show if the king were present.

---

3 **angel** ['eɪndʒəl] messenger of God – 5 **curse** the cause of harm and trouble; evil *(Fluch)*

Act Four

A dark cave

The time had come. In a dark cave somewhere in the middle of Scotland the three witches were dancing round the cauldron, putting all sorts of disgusting things into the pot, singing: “Double, double, toil and trouble; fire burn and cauldron bubble!”

Hecate dropped in for a few moments to make sure that all was well, and congratulated the witches on their powerful brew. The next visitor was Macbeth.

“What are you secret, black and midnight creatures up to?” he asked, looking at the cauldron with suspicion.

“A deed without a name,” was the only reply he got.

Remembering the reason why he had come, he demanded answers to his questions.

“Would you rather hear the answers from our mouths or from our master’s?” asked the first witch.

“Call them, let me see them!” demanded brave Macbeth.

More disgusting things were added to the brew and the fire, and a head appeared in the air with the message: “Macbeth! Beware Macduff; beware the Thane of Fife!” Before Macbeth could ask any more questions, the apparition was gone.

It was replaced by a more powerful apparition: a child covered in blood. The message of this apparition was that Macbeth should be “bloody, bold and resolute” because, it said, no man born of a woman would ever harm him.

Encouraged by this prophecy, Macbeth asked for more. But the next apparition worried him: it was of a child wearing a crown and carrying a tree. But the child’s message was comforting enough:

---

cave natural hole in a cliff or rock face – 2 **cauldron** [ˈkɔːldrən] very large cooking pot – 3 **disgusting** causing strong dislike; making one feel sick – 4 **toil** hard work – **to bubble** when water boils, the steam bubbles out – 6 **brew** drink made by heating the ingredients *(Gebräu)* – 11 **to demand** to ask very strongly – 17 **beware** [bɪˈweə] watch out for danger coming from sb or s.th. – 19 **apparition** [ˌæpəˈrɪʃn] ghost; unreal vision *(Erscheinung)* – 22 **resolute** [ˈrezəluːt] firm; not changing one’s ideas or course of action – 23 **to harm** to do damage to

"Macbeth will never be defeated until Birnam Wood shall march against him up the high hill of Dunsinane."

"That will never be!" said Macbeth with a laugh. "Trees can't be ordered around. Trees can't walk! But tell me," and here he hesitated, for this was the most important question of all. "Shall Banquo's descendants ever reign in this kingdom?"

At first the witches were unwilling to show him more, but at last he persuaded them, and what they showed him horrified him: no less than eight crowned kings appear one after the other, followed by a smiling Banquo.

"What! Is this so?" was all that Macbeth could say.

"Aye, sir, all this is so," said the first witch before she and her sisters disappeared. At that moment Lennox came into the cave, looking for the king, with the news that Macduff had fled to England and thus escaped from the certain death which Macbeth had been planning for him.

Macbeth was furious. "He may have gone," he said. "But I'll attack his castle and kill his wife, his children and all his relatives. And I'll do it soon, before my anger cools!"

He had hired killers before, and he would do so again.

Macduff's castle at Fife

If Lady Macduff had known what Macbeth was planning, she and her family would have followed her husband south as fast as horses would take them. But she suspected nothing.

Even when the Earl of Ross brought the news that her husband had fled, thus automatically turning himself into a traitor; even when a messenger came hurrying by to warn her that her life was in danger.

Where could she go? Her husband was now a traitor. He had left his land, his titles, her and her children behind. Only when the murderers themselves pushed their way into the castle at Fife,

---

6 **to reign** [reɪn] *here:* to be king or queen *(als König oder Königin regieren)* – 12 **aye** [aɪ] yes (old form)

killing her eldest son in cold blood, did she run off crying "Murderer!" The murderers quickly followed her...

Now it was clear to all that not even innocent women and children were safe in Macbeth's Scotland. The situation had become worse than ever before. Something would have to be done – and soon.

King Edward's palace in England

Macduff had meanwhile reached the court of the English king Edward in London, where he met Malcolm. Very much the man of action, he could not hide his disappointment when he discovered that Duncan's son did not seem ready to fight his father's murderer and free Scotland from the tyrant.

The two men did not seem to trust each other.

"You were Macbeth's friend," said Malcolm. "If things are as bad as you say, why did you leave your wife and children in Scotland? I'll do what I can when the time comes, but I don't really feel that I would make a better king than Macbeth. And don't forget that tyrants sometimes become more liberal with time."

"Bleed, bleed, poor country!" cried Macduff, staring at the young Malcolm in disbelief. "You're afraid! A coward! And as for me, I'm not the villain you think I am."

"It's not that I don't believe you," Malcolm went on. "And I've been offered an army of several thousand men by the English king. It's just that I don't trust myself: you know my weakness – women. If I became king, I'm afraid that no woman would be safe from my lust."

Macduff looked at him in horror and disgust. "Surely there are enough women in Scotland to satisfy your lust without our wives and daughters being in danger?" he suggested.

"But what about my love of money?" Malcolm went on. "I might want to steal other men's lands and goods. And the more I got, the more I would want. I know my weak nature only too well."

---

20 **villain** ['vɪlən] bad or evil person – 23 **weakness** *here:* fault or defect of character – 25 **lust** strong (often sexual) desire to possess

"Never mind that," continued Macduff, beginning to wonder whether Malcolm was indeed fit to govern Scotland at all. "There's plenty of land in Scotland. One or two weaknesses won't necessarily make you a bad king. What about your good qualities?"

"I have none," was Malcolm's simple answer.

"God help Scotland!" cried Macduff. "Your father was a good man, your mother spent more time on her knees in church than on her feet! I can see it's no good talking to you. Goodbye!"

Malcolm grabbed his arm. "Just a minute, Macduff. I was only testing you. Now I know I can trust you. Nothing I said about myself just now is true. I am at your service to help my poor country. And I've got even better news for you: before you arrived, Earl Siward of Northumberland was about to march to Scotland with ten thousand men. We can join him now."

Macduff was thunderstruck – and very pleased. He shook Malcolm's hand. There was still time to free Scotland from the tyrant Macbeth and put a rightful king on the throne.

Just at that moment, the Earl of Ross came into the courtyard, tired from his long ride south. He brought bad news about Scotland.

"Now is the time to return," he urged. "If people saw you and Malcolm, they would pick up their weapons and follow you – I think even the women would fight to be rid of their sufferings!"

"We have Siward and ten thousand soldiers," said Malcolm. "There's no better general than him anywhere in the world."

But the news the Earl of Ross brought for Macduff about his family was the worst of all. His wife and children murdered. All his servants killed. Macduff was terribly shocked.

"Turn your grief into anger," urged Malcolm.

"Right," said Macduff. "The sooner I have Macbeth at the end of my sword, the better."

"That's what I wanted to hear," said Malcolm. "We're ready to fight now. Let's say goodbye to King Edward without waiting another moment! Macbeth's time has come! It's a long night that has no day to follow it!"

---

15 **thunderstruck** very surprised – 17 **rightful** correct according to law – 21 **to urge** [ɜːdʒ] to use strong arguments to make sb do something

Act Five

Macbeth's castle at Dunsinane

Strange things were happening in Scotland. Macbeth had marched off with his army to fight Siward and Malcolm, leaving his wife at Dunsinane Castle. But Lady Macbeth could find no peace. She could not sleep in the dark: she needed a burning candle beside her bed and had started to walk in her sleep. One of her ladies-in-waiting saw her get out of bed, unlock her writing-desk, take out a piece of paper, write something on it, read it, seal it and return to bed.

The lady-in-waiting was so worried that she called a doctor. But although they watched and waited two nights in a row, nothing happened. On the third night, however, Lady Macbeth appeared, carrying a candle. Her eyes were open, but, as the lady-in-waiting said in a whisper to the surprised doctor, her senses were closed.

While the two watched, Lady Macbeth put down the candle and began rubbing her hands. The doctor looked at her closely. She was not really rubbing her hands, she seemed to be washing them. Washing them clean of what? She answered the doctor's question as she began to talk in her sleep: "There's still a spot here. Out, damned spot! We needn't fear anyone who knows what we've done when we have power in the kingdom! Who would have thought the old man had so much blood in him?"

Suddenly the doctor realized what Lady Macbeth was doing. She was washing blood off her hands! Whose blood? Who was 'the old man'? Could she mean King Duncan?

"The Thane of Fife had a wife," she went on. "Where is she now? Will these hands never be clean? Here's the smell of blood still! All the perfumes of Arabia will not sweeten this little hand!" She gave a deep sigh and continued, as if speaking to her husband: "Wash your hands; put on your nightgown; don't look so pale. I

---

9 **lady-in-waiting** woman servant who looks after the needs of a queen – 13 **sense** we have five senses: sight, hearing, touch, taste and smell – 15 **to rub** to quickly move one's hand across s.th. (often one's other hand) several times – 29 **nightgown** ['naɪtɡaʊn] dress worn in bed

tell you yet again, Banquo's buried; he cannot come out of his grave. There's knocking at the gate. Come, give me your hand: what's done cannot be undone. To bed, to bed, to bed." And with those words she walked slowly back into her bedroom.

"There's nothing I can do to help her," said the doctor sadly. "It's a priest she needs, not a doctor. Look after her – and make sure she doesn't have anything that she could hurt herself with: anything sharp – a knife, a dagger, anything like that. Good night. And don't tell anyone what we've seen!"

Open country near Dunsinane

Not far from Dunsinane Castle, Macbeth's army was preparing to meet Malcolm, Siward and their troops. Morale among the king's army was not high. Several officers were standing around, exchanging bits of news or gossip.

"The English army led by Malcolm, his uncle Siward and Macduff is quite close now," said Menteith.

"We'll meet them near Birnam Wood," said Angus, not realizing the importance of this place to Macbeth, who would remember that one of the apparitions had told him that he would not be defeated until Birnam Wood came to Dunsinane.

"Does anyone know if Donalbain is with his brother?" asked Caithness. Lennox told him he was certain Donalbain was not, for a spy had given him a list of all the noblemen in Malcolm's army.

"What is the king doing?" asked Menteith.

"He's turning Dunsinane Castle into a fortress," replied Caithness. "Some say he's mad. Others, who hate him less, say that he is brave in his anger."

"Now he feels the blood of his secret murders sticking on his hands," said Angus, in a quiet voice. "We only obey his orders – let's be honest: we don't feel any love towards this tyrant. He has broken his word too often."

---

3 **undone** not done – 11 **morale** [mə'rɑ:l] confidence and optimism of a group of people, esp. of soldiers – 13 **gossip** talk, often uniformed or untrue, about other people's affairs – 24 **fortress** very strong castle

"Well, let's march on," said Caithness. "We must all obey the king and give our lives for him, if necessary."

"Only as many lives as necessary," said Lennox half-heartedly.

And slowly they and their army marched off towards Birnam.

Macbeth's castle

In a room in Dunsinane Castle, Macbeth was growing angry at the pessimistic reports about the approaching English army. The news that this army was ten thousand strong sent him into a rage, and the messenger fled in terror at the king's anger.

Remembering the apparitions he had seen in the cave and their prophecies, however, he found some comfort.

"The apparitions said that I should be bloody, bold and resolute because no man born of a woman would ever harm me. They said I would never be defeated until Birnam Wood marched against me up the high hill of Dunsinane! That will never be!" said Macbeth with a laugh. "Trees can't be ordered around. Trees can't walk! And Malcolm, like all men, was born of a woman. So what am I worried about? I'm not afraid! I'll fight until they cut my flesh from my bones. Seyton!" he shouted to one of his officers. "Give me my armour."

"It isn't needed yet," replied the astonished Seyton, but Macbeth was eager to be bloody, bold and resolute.

He ordered Seyton to send more riders out into the countryside around. "Hang those that talk of fear!" he ordered.

Just then, the doctor who had been looking after Lady Macbeth came in.

"How is your patient, doctor?" Macbeth asked anxiously.

"She isn't really ill, my lord. She is imagining things. She sees things that keep her awake at night."

"You doctors can cure a diseased body. Why can't you cure a diseased mind? Is there no medicine that will rub out a sorrow

---

7 **rage** [reɪdʒ] very strong anger – 17 **flesh** muscle on a living body – 19 **armour** ['ɑːmə] pieces of metal worn on the body to protect it in battle

from the memory, remove the worries from the brain? Nothing to make a heavy heart lighter?"

"Only the patient herself can do that," the doctor replied. "I cannot."

"To hell with medicine, then," replied the king angrily as he reached for his armour and weapons. "Do what you can for her, doctor. If you could make her well again, I would pay you generously. As for the English, I'm not afraid of them! I won't fear death till Birnam forest marches on Dunsinane. Doctors!" he laughed scornfully. "Don't you have any drug that could rid the country of the English army? A purgative? Ha ha! Rhubarb? Senna?"

The doctor was disgusted. The man must be mad – his wife certainly was! Driven mad by feelings of guilt at bloody crimes which she and her husband must have planned and carried out together! A purgative for the English? If this was the king's idea of a joke, the wise old doctor thought, then it was in extremely bad taste. And as for generous payment, he would never come back to Dunsinane Castle if only he could escape now! He wished he had never come.

Near Birnam Wood

By the time the English army had reached Birnam, it had received unexpected help. Most of Macbeth's officers had deserted to the enemy! Menteith, Caithness, Angus and Lennox, who only hours before had talked about only following orders and doing their duty must have listened to their consciences at last.

---

1 **memory** the things one remembers *(Gedächtnis)* – 10 **scornfully** showing or feeling that someone or something deserves no respect *(höhnisch)* – 11 **purgative** ['pɜ:gətɪv] medicine or substance used to clean the inside of the body from the stomach downwards – **rhubarb** ['ru:bɑ:b] plant with long stalks that are eaten as a fruit dessert and which has the effects of a mild purgative – 12 **senna** dried leaves of the cassia plant used as a laxative – 14 **guilt** [gɪlt] sense of having done something wrong

There had been too many innocent people murdered, too much bloodshed even for them. Duty be damned! What Scotland needed was peace, and the only way to achieve this was to free Scotland from the tyrant Macbeth.

"Cousins," said Malcolm encouragingly, for many of these noblemen were indeed close relatives of the royal family, "I hope our homes will soon be safe!"

"We're sure of that!" replied Menteith.

"What's the name of that wood over there?" asked Earl Siward, unfamiliar with the territory.

"Birnam wood," said Menteith.

Suddenly Malcolm had an idea. "Tell each soldier to cut off a branch and to carry it in front of him. Then the enemy won't be able to see exactly how many of us are coming!"

"Good idea," said several of the soldiers at once, and they began cutting off branches – branches large enough to hide the troops if they all marched close together. Large enough to look like a forest on the march ...

"No sign of resistance," said Siward as they approached the castle. "Macbeth is safe inside! We'll surround the castle and wait. He'll have to come out some time!"

"The only soldiers Macbeth has got," said Malcolm, "are slaves and paid mercenaries. Their heart is not in it."

Siward, the experienced soldier and man of action, was not quite so optimistic. "We'll see," he said. "There are certain things that can only be decided by cold steel." And he put his hand confidently on his sword.

Macbeth's castle

"Hang out our flags on the outside walls," said Macbeth to Seyton when he heard that the English army was approaching. "Our castle is strong enough now! Let them stand around outside until

---

2 **Duty be damned!** [dæmd] To hell with duty! – 19 **resistance** [rɪ'zɪstəns] opposition, fighting back *(Widerstand)* – 23 **mercenary** ['mɜːsɪnərɪ] hired soldier who fights for a foreign country *(Söldner)* – 27 **confidently** full of trust and optimism

they get so hungry or sick that they have to leave. If our soldiers had not deserted, we would have gone out to meet the enemy, face to face, and beaten them back home!"

The king had put his armour on and was preparing to go out with Seyton and other soldiers to watch the enemy from the castle walls, when he heard a sudden sound of women crying.

"What noise is that?" he asked angrily. Seyton went out to see, and returned with bad news.

"The queen, my lord, is dead."

"Dead? What a time to die! Couldn't she have waited until tomorrow?" was all that the king could say.

Seyton and the others were horrified. Did the king have no feelings?

"Tomorrow," said the king again, and, seeming to forget that he was not alone, began to express his deepest feelings about life and death: life goes on in a meaningless way, one tomorrow after the other, creeping slowly from day to day to the end of time! Since the beginning of time, our past actions have shown fools the way to dusty death!

"Life!" he muttered, but in a voice loud enough for all to hear him. "Life's only a walking shadow, a bad actor who walks up and down the stage noisily playing his part for a short time and then is heard no more. The meaning of life?" he gave a bitter laugh and, looking up at last, realized that he, like some actor, also had an audience of astonished, open-mouthed soldiers, many of whom would lose their own lives that very day. "Life? Ha! Life is a story told by an idiot, full of sound and fury, meaning – nothing!"

There was a long, embarrassed silence.

At last the silence was broken by a messenger hurrying in with the latest news. He bowed to the king, opened his mouth, but no words came out. He closed it again quickly and looked at the ground.

---

17 **to creep, crept, crept** to move very slowly, often on hands and feet – 20 **to mutter** to speak in a low voice that even people nearby cannot understand – 25 **audience** ['ɔ:dɪəns] people who go to watch a play, hear a concert etc. – 27 **fury** ['fjʊərɪ] violent anger – 28 **embarrassed** feeling awkward or unhappy about a situation in which one feels out of place

Seyton:	The queen, my lord, is dead.
Macbeth:	She should have died hereafter; There would have been a time for such a word. To-morrow, and to-morrow, and to-morrow Creeps in this petty pace from day to day To the last syllable of recorded time; And all our yesterdays have lighted fools The way to dusty death. Out, out, brief candle! Life's but a walking shadow, a poor player That struts and frets his hour upon the stage And then is heard no more. It is a tale Told by an idiot, full of sound and fury Signifying nothing.

"You came to use your tongue!" Macbeth shouted. "Your story! Quickly!"

"I don't know how to tell you what I saw, my lord," said the messenger. "I was up on the hill, watching out for the enemy. I looked towards Birnam, and it seemed to me that the wood itself was moving!"

Macbeth suddenly went pale. "Liar and slave!"

"If I'm a liar," came the brave reply, "you can do what you like to me, my lord. Go outside and look! Three miles away you can see it coming – a moving forest!"

"If you're lying," growled the king, "I'll tie you alive to the nearest tree until you die of hunger! If what you say is true, you can do the same to me!"

At last Macbeth realized the terrible truth behind the prophecies he had heard in the witches' cave. A truth which Banquo had quickly recognised: they had a double meaning! At first he had thought nothing could harm him. He now recognized the awful truth: "Fear not till Birnam wood comes to Dunsinane" he muttered. "And now a wood comes towards Dunsinane! This is

---

1 **tongue** [tʌŋ] important organ of speech located in the mouth behind the teeth – 7 **liar** ['laɪə] person who does not tell the truth – 11 **to growl** [graʊl] to make a noise like an angry dog

witchcraft! To arms – and out! It's no use waiting here, no use trying to flee. I'm beginning to get tired of life! At least we'll die with our armour on and swords in our hands!"

And out they marched to meet the English army. Perhaps Macbeth was hoping that the final prophecy would not have a double meaning: that no man born of woman could ever harm him. That thought might have cheered him up a little. But perhaps he had forgotten it. It was all the same to him now.

Outside Dunsinane Castle

When Malcolm's army reached the castle the soldiers threw down the branches behind which they had been hiding and showed themselves for what they were.

"You and your son can lead the first attack," said Malcolm to Earl Siward. "Macduff and I will do whatever else needs to be done."

Malcolm gave the signal for the battle to begin. Trumpets sounded, and the two armies moved slowly towards each other.

On the battlefield

Macbeth was a good fighter. Even more so because he had at last remembered the final prophecy. 'Is there any man who was not born of a woman?' he asked himself. 'Impossible! I have nothing to fear!'

Was it chance that brought Macbeth and Siward's son together in close fighting? They had never met, so young Siward asked the unknown knight.

"What is your name?"

"You'll be afraid to hear it!"

"No. Not if it's a hotter name than any in hell!"

---

1 **witchcraft** the use of magic by a witch or witches – **to arms!** old-fashioned order to begin fighting – 22 **knight** [naɪt] soldier, often a nobleman, who wore armour in battle *(Ritter)*

"My name's Macbeth," came the answer.

"The devil himself couldn't speak a name that I hate more!"

"No, nor a name more terrible!" cried Macbeth, and they began to fight.

Though young Siward fought well, he was not able to fight better than the old soldier Macbeth. Pulling his sword from the young man's dying body, Macbeth smiled with satisfaction.

"You were born of a woman. I smile at swords and weapons carried by men of woman born!" And with that he marched off to another part of the battlefield. He was keeping a sharp eye open for Macduff. For it was only now that he remembered the first prophecy in the witches' cave: 'Macbeth, beware Macduff!' If Macbeth feared anybody, it was the man whose family he had had brutally murdered.

But Macduff was looking for him. He dearly wanted to kill Macbeth himself. 'If someone else kills the tyrant,' he thought, 'the ghosts of my dead wife and children will never be at peace. I'll kill no one else! If I can't kill Macbeth, I'll put my sword away unused!'

Hearing the sound of battle coming from another direction he moved towards it, his sword in his hand.

Though the fighting outside the castle went on, the castle itself had surrendered. The battle was almost over. Siward and Malcolm, satisfied with their day's work, walked in through the open gate.

Another part of the battlefield

The castle had surrendered. The English army had been far too large for Macbeth and his soldiers. But still the killing went on. Macbeth thought about suicide as a possible way out but decided not to play "the Roman fool and die on my own sword".

Suddenly a well-known voice behind him shouted: "Turn, hell-hound, turn!"

It was Macduff.

"Get away from me!" cried Macbeth. "I've been keeping out of your way for a good reason. I don't want to have to kill you. I've spilt enough of your family's blood already!"

But Macduff came straight at him, and they began to fight.

"You're wasting your time!" cried Macbeth as they fought. "My life is protected by a charm. No man born of woman can harm me!"

"Ha!" cried Macduff. "Your charm won't help you now! I was not born the normal way! My mother died while I was being born. The doctors cut her open to save my life – and I lived!"

"Damn you!" cried Macbeth. "And damn those witches and apparitions who told me truths with a double sense! I won't fight you, Macduff!"

"Then surrender, coward!" said Macduff scornfully. "And live like a rare monster in a zoo – we'll put you in a cage with a sign at the bottom: 'Here you may see the tyrant'!"

"I won't surrender!" cried Macbeth. "To kiss the ground before young Malcolm's feet and to be mocked and laughed at by the crowd!"

So, though the battle was almost over, the two men fought on.

Some time later, when the fighting had at last stopped, Malcolm and Earl Siward came out of the castle to look for missing officers.

"Macduff is missing, and your noble son," said Malcolm to Siward. But Ross knew what had happened to young Siward.

"Your son, my lord, has died like a soldier. He was still young – only able to prove he was a man by dying like a man."

"Then he is dead?" asked Siward, sadly.

Ross nodded. Remembering that this had been his son's first battle, Siward had an equally important question.

"Where was he wounded? At the front or in the back?"

"At the front."

"Why, then he's God's soldier! If I had as many sons as I have hairs, I would not wish them a fairer death!" said the brave old soldier. "Here comes better news!" cried Siward, seeing Macduff walking up to them. He was holding Macbeth's head in his hand. "Hail, king!" were Macduff's first words. "Here is the tyrant's head! Scotland is free at last!"
Seeing that Malcolm was surrounded by most of the noblemen of Scotland, Macduff went down on one knee, crying: "Hail, King of Scotland!"

---

3 **charm** magic spell or talisman used to bring good luck – 15 **to mock** to make fun of

The cry was repeated by the other thanes, who also bowed before their new king.

Malcolm was so happy that he honoured all the Thanes present by giving them the old English title of Earl: “You are the first men that ever Scotland in such an honour named,” as he put it.

“Now that the tyrant Macbeth is dead – that butcher and his devilish queen who, they say, took her own life – we have a lot to do. Let us call home our exiled friends who fled from tyranny and start living normal lives again. Thank you all for what you have done. I would like to invite you all to my coronation at Scone.“

And this time, all the noblemen of Scotland and their wives and children came to the new king's happy coronation.

---

8 **exiled** ['eksaɪld] living outside one's country for political reasons

Epilogue

So peace returned once again to Scotland. Malcolm III was crowned at Scone Abbey in 1057, founding the powerful House of Canmore, which ruled Scotland for two hundred years.

And Banquo's son Fleance? And the eight crowned heads in the vision which Macbeth saw in the witches' cave? Almost a thousand years have passed and Scotland is still waiting for them!

J.D. Mackie's book 'A History of Scotland' mentions neither Banquo nor Fleance. So at least this one prophecy of the three witches was wrong! Or did Shakespeare just invent these characters?

And Macbeth, it seems, was a good king who ruled Scotland for seventeen years!

But nobody pays good money to see a play about a good king, thought Shakespeare. Blood and thunder – that's what people come to my theatre to see! And he was certainly right about that.

Shakespeares Tragödie wird Szene um Szene nacherzählt. Besonders bekannte Passagen erscheinen in der Originalversion. Die Lektüre ist ab der 9. Klasse einsetzbar, eignet sich jedoch auch für Grundkurse.

9 783125 305106
510-1

Klett